Bach: The Keyboard Works

Bach: The Keyboard Works

Toccata & Fugue in D minor, *BWV 565*

English Suite No. 1 in A, *BWV 806*

Partita No. 5 in G, *BWV 629*

"Little" Fugue in G minor, *BWV 678*

Italian Concerto in F minor, *BWV 971*

TEXT BY DAVID FOIL

BLACK DOG & LEVENTHAL PUBLISHERS
NEW YORK

Published by
Black Dog & Leventhal Publishers Inc.
151 West 19th Street
New York, NY 10011

Distributed by
Workman Publishing Company
708 Broadway
New York, NY 10003

Designed by Martin Lubin and Allison Russo

Special thanks to Judith Dupré

Book manufactured in Hong Kong

ISBN: 1-884822-42-8

FOREWORD

*J*ohann Sebastian Bach posessed a brilliant ability to interweave aesthetic expression and melody with the highly constrictive rules of Baroque structure, harmony, and counterpoint. The results are works of genius and beauty. In this volume you will be able to read and learn about Johann Sebastian Bach, the man and the composer; you will better understand the importance, the meaning, and the structure of his great keyboard works; and you can enjoy and listen to the music as you read.

Play the compact disc included on the inside front cover of this book and follow along with the musical commentary and analysis. Please note that the times of the relevant musical passages are noted for your convenience.

Enjoy this book and enjoy the music.

Johann Sebastian Bach

"There is nothing so remarkable about it," Johann Sebastian Bach is reputed to have said about playing the organ. "One need only hit the right keys at the right time, and the instrument plays itself."

There is something so apt—and so extraordinary—about that quotation that one hopes it is accurate. Music has never produced another genius whose devotion to his art was as methodical, as lucid, and as energetic in its evolution as Johann Sebastian Bach's. His enduring work as a composer is the bedrock of the modern tradition in Western music. Its visionary innovations and aesthetic quality have been both lesson and inspiration to musicians for the better part of three centuries.

Hyperbole is nothing new to a discussion of Bach. Beethoven called him "the immortal god of harmony." Rossini stated that "if Beethoven is a prodigy among men . . . Bach is a miracle of God." Wagner described his work as "the most stupendous miracle in all of music." Debussy considered him "a benevolent god, to whom musicians should offer a prayer before setting to work so that they may be preserved from mediocrity." After hearing an organ work of Bach's, the German philosopher Johann Wolfgang von Goethe wrote, "It is as though eternal harmony were conversing with itself, as it may have happened in God's bosom shortly before He created the world."

But the reality of Bach's life and career—or at least what we have been able to discover about them—does not square with these heroic assessments. His life was that of a solid German Lutheran burgher, one who would make that statement about hitting the right keys at the right time. If he was ever aware of what he achieved, there is no evidence that he said as much. He was too busy to ponder his place in the continuum of music—too busy doing his job, fulfilling his numerous obligations, and raising his enormous family. A devout Christian, he made it clear at all times that his music was written to the greater glory of God. But he was hardly the formidable saint some would have us believe. Contemporary reports describe him as a big-hearted, robust man who presided over a teeming household. He smoked a pipe and took delight in the fact that, while living in Leipzig, he got his beer tax-free because he was a church official. He tuned his own instruments and knew how they operated. He had a temper and plenty of ambition. He liked making money and worked hard. All of these qualities create a picture of Bach as a responsible, fully engaged man of his time. Lurking behind that image, however, was the soul of a genius.

His Life

Bach was born into a family of provincial musicians in the German town of Eisenach in 1685. His father, Johann Ambrosius Bach, was the town organist and musician. An orphan by the time he was ten, Johann Sebastian was sent with his brother Johann Jacob to live with his elder brother Johann Christoph in Ohrdruf, where he appears to have had his first serious musical training. (The name Johann was a tradition in the Bach family: all six of Johann Ambrosius's sons carried the first name of Johann, as did all four sons of his brother Johann Christoph. There were many Johannas as well.) At the age of fifteen, Johann Sebastian left Ohrdruf for Lüneberg, some two hundred miles away, where he studied for three years as chorister and organist under Georg Böhm. In the spring of 1703, at the age of eighteen, he secured his first position as a musician in the Weimar court. Later that summer he was named organist at the Neuekirche in Arnstadt.

For the next twenty years Bach moved between church jobs and court appointments in the German provinces before settling, in 1723, in Leipzig, where he would spend the rest of his life in charge of music at St. Thomas Church. In his first position at Arnstadt, and later at a church in Mühlhausen, Bach began to explore the virtuosic potential of the organ and the family of keyboard instruments, principally the harpsichord and the clavichord. In 1708 he was appointed organist and court musician to the ducal court at Weimar, where he remained for eleven years. A promotion of sorts came in 1717, when he was named *Kapellmeister* (musical director) to

Prince Leopold of Cöthen, a move that so enraged Duke Wilhelm Ernst of Weimar that he had Bach thrown into jail for a month. Cöthen was the ideal job, one that Bach always would regret leaving, for Prince Leopold was a skillful amateur musician who recognized the greatness in his new *Kapellmeister.* During his years in Weimar and especially in Cöthen, Bach was inspired to write the bulk of his orchestral and instrumental music.

When he was reluctantly awarded the position in Leipzig—the candidate chosen over him withdrew at the last minute—he shifted the emphasis of

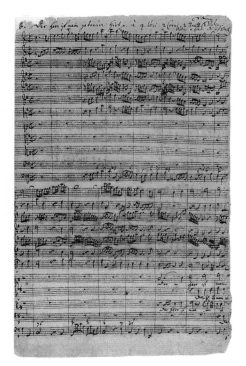

his work to choral music. In the final twenty-seven years of his life, he composed more than 250 sacred cantatas, as well as the *St. Matthew Passion,* the Easter and Christmas oratorios, the motets, and a variety of mass settings, for St. Thomas Church and its sister church. It was not a satisfying experience; Bach suffered at the hands of an unfriendly administration. He also had to make do with the inept musical forces available to him, such as a local hack, Picander, who wrote cantata texts so banal that it is a wonder Bach managed to set them to such sublime music. Bach endured these aggravations

Page 1 from Cantata 112 *of 1731. Bach composed more than 250 sacred cantatas in his lifetime.*

because of the relative stature of the job and his need to provide for his growing family. In 1733 he sought some relief in a bid to be named composer to the Royal Saxon Chapel, submitting what he called "a trifling example of my skill." That turned out to be the epic first two movements of the Mass in B Minor, a monumental work he would complete five years later. Bach was denied the position and never heard the Mass performed in its entirety; the world premiere took place in Berlin, in two parts, in 1834 and 1835, some eighty-five years after his death in 1750.

Bach's duties in Leipzig extended beyond composition and the musical preparation of services. He also had to teach in the choir school, a task for which he must have been well prepared: Bach fathered twenty children during his two marriages. His first wife, his cousin Maria Barbara Bach, was the mother of seven of his children; she died in 1720. A year later he married Anna Magdalena Wilcken, the daughter of the court trumpeter at Cöthen, who gave birth to an additional thirteen children. Only ten of the Bach offspring lived past childhood, but four of the surviving sons became notable composers.

During his lifetime Bach was known and respected, primarily as an organist, throughout Germany. The music he wrote had little exposure outside the immediate circumstances of its composition, however, and it was sometimes dismissed as being either old-fashioned or merely serviceable, whether the work in question was a church cantata or a virtuoso instrumental piece. Bach was relentless in his efforts to please the aristocracy, even in the face of indifference. The Margrave of Brandenburg paid no attention to the six concertos Bach sent him, accompanied by an absurdly flattering note, in an effort to curry favor. The margrave's orchestra was too small to play the *Brandenburg Concertos,* and the score was tossed into his library, where it

remained until after his death, when some of the library's contents were sold. One of Bach's students, realizing what he had found, bought the manuscript for a trivial amount.

Bach's Children

Who were all those other Bachs?

Wilhelm Friedemann Bach (1710–1784), the eldest of Bach's sons, was known as the Halle Bach. After training with his father, he studied mathematics, philosophy, and law at the University of Leipzig before deciding on a career in music. Beginning with a post in Dresden, he held a succession of church positions, most notably a turbulent eighteen-year stint at the Liebfrauenkirche in Halle. In 1774, he moved to Berlin, where he spent the rest of his life, which ended in poverty and bitterness. Regarded for a time as the finest Baroque organist in Germany after his father, Wilhelm Friedemann led an unhappy, unstable life, dogged by his unyielding personality and lack of discipline. His music is interesting and attractive, but not especially memorable, and his miseries reduced him to scandalous desperation—he is known to have claimed some of his august father's music as his own, and even to have signed Johann Sebastian Bach's name to one of his own works.

Carl Philipp Emanuel Bach (1714–1788) is the most respected of Bach's four sons who achieved prominence as composers. The second of Bach's surviving sons (his mother was Maria Barbara), he is known as the

The artist and his family. Bach fathered
twenty children during his two marriages.

Berlin Bach or the Hamburg Bach. He was a student of his father's at the St. Thomas School in Leipzig before studying law at the universities in Leipzig and Frankfurt. He returned to music in 1738, taking a position two years later in the Berlin court orchestra of Frederick the Great of Prussia, who was an amateur composer himself. Carl Philipp Emanuel remained there, chafing under the conservative tastes of the Prussian king, until 1768, when he was called to become the musical director of five churches and cantor of the Latin school

Carl Philipp Emanuel Bach (1714–1788) was the most respected of Bach's four musical sons.

called the Johanneum, all in Hamburg, positions he held for the rest of his life. Carl Philipp Emanuel's music—a radical departure from his father's—fully embraced the style of "intimate expressiveness" that had become the German answer to the dazzling works of the French Rococo. His influence during his lifetime was considerable, and Haydn in particular had great respect for him.

Johann Christoph Friedrich Bach (1732–1795), the ninth of Bach's sons (his mother was Bach's second wife, Anna Magdalena), was known as the Bückeberg Bach. He trained initially with his father before deciding to study law at the University of Leipzig in 1749. The following year, after his father died, he reconsidered and took a position as a chamber musician in Bückeberg at the court of Count Wilhelm of Schaumburg-Lippe. He remained there for the rest of his life, eventually becoming the court's musical director and composer. A keyboard virtuoso, Johann Christoph Friedrich wrote a large body of music—none of it innovative but all of it polished and elegant—that was influenced by his half brother Carl Philipp Emanuel and, eventually, by Haydn and Mozart. He outlived all his brothers.

Johann Christian Bach (1735–1782), the eleventh and youngest surviving son of J. S. Bach and his second wife, was also known as John Christian Bach and the London Bach. He received early instruction from his father and, after the elder Bach's death in 1750, moved to Berlin to complete his studies with his half brother Carl Philipp Emanuel. Johann Christian eventually left for Italy, where he was briefly an organist at the Cathedral in Milan. He also composed operas, many of them in the Italian style. In 1762 he traveled to London, where he spent the rest of his life. He took an early interest in Mozart, and Mozart liked and respected his work as well, using thematic material of Johann Christian's in his own compositions. Johann

Bach's youngest son, Johann Christian Bach (1735–1782), wrote in the expressive manner of his time.

Christian's music, and there is a great deal of it, departed from the essential purity of his father's. Instead, he absorbed inspiration, along with Carl Philipp Emanuel and Haydn and Mozart, from the expressive, *galant* manner of the time—the spark that would ignite the Classical era.

A fifth brother, **Johann Gottfried Bernhard (1715–1739),** made several stabs at a career as an organist with the continuing assistance of his father. Impatient, immature, and irresponsible, he disappeared to die in obscurity at the age of twenty-four—a black sheep in a family of high achievers.

Bach's four surviving daughters met with the unhappy fate of bourgeois girls whose families were incapable of providing them with attractive dowries. His daughter Regina Susanna, born in 1742, lived until 1809, longer than any of Bach's children. When admirers of Bach, including Beethoven, discovered that she was living in Vienna in abject poverty, they created a fund to allow her to live out her days in relative comfort.

Bach and Handel

We can compare J. S. Bach's career to that of the German Baroque era's other great master, George Frideric Handel. Born the same year as Bach—within a few weeks, in fact—Handel lived in a town just sixty miles away from Eisenach. The coincidences continued until the end of their lives: Both went blind and were treated by the same celebrated doctor (whose remedy may have hastened both of their deaths, which occurred nine years apart). Bach and Handel never met, though Bach earnestly tried to make that happen. Handel left Germany early in his career, picking up the influences of Italy during his travels there, and found fame and fortune in England. He was a celebrity when he returned to his homeland, and Bach was a mere choirmaster whom he had no particular desire to meet. Bach, willing to go anywhere and meet anyone who could teach him something, never managed to meet Handel despite his efforts.

Together Bach and Handel brought the German Baroque era in music to a glorious close, pointing the way to the innovations of the Classical era. They were two very different composers. Handel was inspired at every turn by the sound of the human voice. Everything he wrote seems to sing, and he is a pivotal figure in the history of opera. Bach considered opera trivial and frivolous. In his case the inspiration always sprang from the keyboard, and his vocal writing, while quite beautiful in its own way, lacks Handel's incomparable fluency. Handel wrote gorgeous melodies, but the technical aspects of composition did not concern him unduly. Though Bach was quite a melodist himself, his command of the technical aspects of music was so expert that he was able to achieve an eloquence that has never been equaled.

George Frideric Handel at the clavier. With Bach, he brought the German Baroque era to a glorious close.

Bach's greatness rests on that achievement, which sometimes

daunts listeners and performers. His genius defines itself in a breathtaking mastery of polyphony, or the simultaneous combination of several individual voices, or musical lines, that move in counterpoint. If that sounds dry and formal, it isn't. Bach could take a minor technical challenge, such as the writing of a fugue, and turn it into a miracle of invention and musical expression. Listen to the "Little" Fugue in G Minor in this collection: The melodic subject is forthright and arresting in its simplicity, sounding off at intervals in the basic manner of a fugue. When the other voices begin to enter, something magical happens, and the sum of the music becomes greater than the whole of its parts. This music isn't *about* anything—it is just a fugue—but we do not have to grasp its technical specifications to enjoy it. The exuberance and imagination of Bach's gift imbue this short, compact exercise, and everything else he wrote, with a charisma and significance that transcend technique.

Perhaps that quotation about hitting the right keys at the right time is not as disingenuous as it sounds. In the larger sense, as a composer and creative spirit, that is exactly what Bach did, and then, as now, the instrument seems to play itself. But Bach was wrong about one thing: It is profoundly remarkable.

The Modern Revival of Bach

Bach's music fell into some obscurity after his death. He was, after all, just a church and court musician for hire, and even some of his sons enjoyed greater fame in cosmopolitan circles than he did. Bach composed music for the moment, not for posterity, as did other composers of the day. Musicology, music criticism, and public performance of music did not exist as they do today, and Bach's scores were considered expendable. However, because Bach had his keyboard works published (at his own expense), they continued to circulate and have an impact. Mozart knew and revered them, and had the warmest admiration for Bach's son Carl Philipp Emanuel. Chopin so worshipped Bach's *The Well-Tempered Clavier* that he composed his Op. 28 *Préludes* in tribute.

Felix Mendelssohn (1809-1847) is credited with the modern revival of interest in Bach's music.

The modern revival of interest in Bach's music dates from 1829, when the twenty-year-old Felix Mendelssohn conducted the historic Leipzig performances of Bach's *St. Matthew Passion*. A reappraisal of Bach's entire oeuvre got under way, and by 1850 the Bach Society was formed to shed as much light as possible on his neglected genius. Emphasis at the time was placed on his vast catalog of choral music; most of Bach's keyboard works, with the exception of the great organ masterpieces, remained outside the active repertoire. Liszt and Busoni made spectacular piano transcriptions of other Bach works (his organ pieces, for instance, and the mighty chaconne from the D Minor Violin Partita), and they became more popular with concert audiences than the original keyboard works.

In the early twentieth century, Wanda Landowska's bold scholarship and persistence resulted in a fresh approach to the keyboard works, particularly for harpsichord, and Albert Schweitzer's organ music and writings on Bach had the same effect on that corner of the repertoire. In the decades since Landowska and Schweitzer were active, the developments have been subtle but telling. There is now a vital school of Bach keyboard performance on historically accurate harpsichords and organs, tuned to pitches Bach might have used, and observing the tempo and dynamic markings that mimic the style of his day.

Wanda Landowska (1879-1959) as a girl. Her bold scholarship resulted in a fresh approach to Bach's keyboard works.

The Performance of Bach

While many aspects of Bach's art are frustratingly elusive, few are as persistent as the question of the proper instrument for performing his keyboard works.

The matter would seem to be easily resolved where the organ is concerned, yet the organs Bach played in his career were highly varied instruments, and he composed his music to exploit their different characteristics. In this age of historically authentic performance of Baroque music, organists seek out the restored instruments Bach is known to have played at various points in his life. When he was in his thirties, Bach's music changed as French and Italian influences began to surface, diffusing the earlier impact of the North German school of organ playing and writing. The North German style is typified by the work of Dietrich Buxtehude, the organ master of Lübeck whom Bach is said to have traveled 260 miles on foot to meet. The organs preferred by the North German virtuosos had a precise, reverberant sound that sometimes bordered on stridency, while the southern influences on Bach's music yielded increased tonal color and a warmer sound.

The ideal Bach sound is probably best produced on organs built by the composer's Saxon contemporary, Gottfried Silberman (1683–1753), reputedly the finest organ builder in that part of what is now Germany. Organ building is a sophisticated art, requiring not only mechanical ingenuity and a musical sensibility, but a subtle grasp of acoustics; Silberman excelled in all three. Though organ building developed still further in Bach's lifetime, the Silberman organ best accommodates the character of Bach's music.

Bach brilliantly exploited the virtuosic potential of the harpsichord. He played on instruments similar to this single manual harpsichord made by P. Gasparro Saberino in the early eighteenth century.

While this may be purely a matter of taste, it does seem that Bach's greatest organ compositions lose very little, and may gain something, when played on a massive Romantic instrument, such as one of those immense, reedy French organs built by Cavaillé-Coll in the late nineteenth century. What is spectacular about the music sounds even more so, and the architecture seems even more imposing. The two organ recordings heard in this collection take what is now considered a mainstream approach to Bach organ performance.

Once we leave the world of the organ, however, we are in the midst of controversy.

Bach had limited exposure to what is known as the piano, whose forerunner first appeared in 1710. We do know that he wished to expand the expressive and dynamic range of the harpsichord—in his lifetime, the preferred keyboard instrument for performance—and that he worked (and fought) with Silberman to develop an enhanced instrument. Strictly speaking, the only historically correct performance of most of his music for this family of instruments can be achieved on a harpsichord or a clavichord. Here the controversy begins.

Pianists who revere Bach's music have taken it up freely on modern concert grand pianos, with the justification that since Bach was pursuing a greater range for the keyboard, he would have embraced such a piano had it been available to him. (After all, pianos we hear today are not identical to the pianos Brahms played on, and there is little argument about Brahms performance style.) Certainly the splendor, scale, and endless imagination of Bach's writing can be enhanced on the modern piano—Maria Tipo's performance of the Partita No. 5 in this collection proves that most eloquently. The problem arises when pianists begin to interpret the music in a Romantic manner inconsistent with performance practices of Bach's day; purists believe the use of extravagantly slow and fast tempos, overly emotional phrasing, and melodramatic dynamics has resulted in the "Wagner-izing" of Bach.

The harpsichord retains a certain stylistic authority: It offers the crisp, pinpoint sound that Bach, as a fine instrument technician and a capable acoustician, sought to achieve. Leonhardt's performance here of the first *English Suite* brilliantly demonstrates this. Fortunately, we live in a world that can offer us both options. This continuing controversy is one that has opened our ears and nourished our awareness of Bach's greatness.

The BWV Index

What does BWV mean when it follows the title of a Bach work?

Bach did not catalog his own music, so his works are not identified by the traditional opus numbers. Such cataloguing, which many composers adopted, did not become standard practice until the nineteenth century. Bach's creative output resulted in a vast catalog that remained in some disarray until the publication—in 1950, the 200th anniversary of the composer's death—of the *Thematisch-Systematisches Verzeichnis der musicalischen Werke von Johann Sebastian Bach (Systematic Thematic Index of Johann Sebastian Bach's Musical Works).*

The shorthand for this academic title is *Bach Werke-Verzeichnis (Index to Bach's Works),* or simply BWV. An individual work will be listed with a BWV number instead of an opus number—the *St. John Passion*, for instance, is BWV 245—much as Köchel numbers have become the standard in identifying the works of Mozart. The BWV numbers sometimes are referred to as Schmieder numbers. The reference is to the musicologist and musical archivist Wolfgang Schmieder (1901–1973), who edited the first edition of the BWV index.

The BWV index includes works that some musicologists believe are of questionable authenticity. This presents a challenge to Bach scholars. The composer left behind little correspondence, no diaries or journals, and shockingly few authentic manuscripts. Several of his most celebrated works, such as the Toccata and Fugue in D Minor, do not exist in autograph manuscripts. These mysteries have created a cottage industry of speculation in the musicology community, some of it provocative, some of it dead-end. The archaeology and study of Bach's work continues, though it is doubtful at this point that anything earth-shattering will materialize to confound what is already known.

The Recordings

TOCCATA AND FUGUE IN D MINOR, BWV 565. Bach's music for organ generally falls into two groups. Most numerous are those created for church use—the chorale preludes and other elaborations on existing chorale melodies, such as Luther's famous chorale *"Ein feste burg"* ("A Mighty Fortress Is Our God"). More famous, though, are what are sometimes called the "free" works, pieces created to display and explore the range of the organ as well as the organist's virtuosity and technical grasp of the instrument.

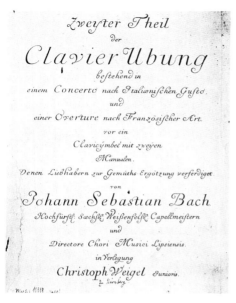

Title page of the Clavier-Übung *(second part), a collection of Bach's keyboard pieces published in 1735.*

The greatest of these free works emerged from an Italian musical form called the toccata, among the oldest of all keyboard forms. Derived from the Italian word *toccare,* meaning "touch," a toccata is intended to display the performer's command of the keyboard in writing that initially sounds free and improvised, and that often leads to subsequent sections in the imitative style of a fugue. The sixteenth-century Italians evolved a five-part format for the toccata, featuring three toccata sections alternating with two fugue sections, and it endured into Bach's time.

As with most musical forms, however, these rules were broken when necessary or were—in Bach's case—rewritten. His toccatas cover a wide and imaginative range of works known individually as preludes and fugues, fantasias and fugues, and toccatas and fugues. The toccata known as Toccata and Fugue in D Minor is probably the single most famous work ever written for the organ. (Purists refer to it as Toccata in D Minor; the longer title is somewhat misleading, since a toccata, in terms of the old five-part format, *is* a toccata and fugue.) In this particular work, Bach restricted himself to three sections: toccata, fugue, and toccata. Its origins are hazy: No autograph manuscript exists, more than one musicologist has doubted its authenticity, and the nature of the writing has even suggested to some that it is an organ transcription of a violin piece.

Generally assumed to be a work by Bach created for the organ, this toccata is thought to have been written before 1708, probably during the two years (1706 and 1707) Bach was in Arnstadt and Mühlhausen. Musicologists who doubt this is Bach's work point out, correctly, that Bach wrote far greater toccatas, built on more interesting thematic material and developed with more skill. But this opinion ignores the inimitable, visceral thrill created by the toccata's opening notes, the musical roller-coaster ride that follows, the vivid fugue section, and the highly dramatic conclusion. Though the Toccata and Fugue in D Minor is most effective in its original form, audiences also know it through a variety of transcriptions, usually for piano or for orchestra. The conductor Leopold Stokowski's monumental orchestral transcription probably introduced the work to its largest audience through its unforgettable use on the soundtrack of Walt Disney's *Fantasia*.

Like a bolt of lightning, the opening line is simple but stunning: A whiplash of an octave trill, followed by a sudden free fall of notes, dramatically rises ([1]0:03) and then drops to another trill ([1]0:07), an octave lower than the first, with a short, sinister response ([1]0:09). Descending even deeper into the bass, all of this is repeated ([1]0:13). After a pause, a startling chord fans out from rumbling pedal tones ([1]0:20). (This particular chord is called a diminished seventh. A seventh chord is any given pitch plus the third, fifth, and seventh notes above it. The diminished seventh chord occurs when all of these intervals of a third are in the minor key, which explains why it has such a grim, unresolved sound.) The soloist resolves the diminished seventh chord into a major chord ([1]0:29). An insistent figure appears ([1]0:31) and is repeated, climbing higher each time, until it begins to tumble wildly ([1] 0:45) into the abyss of another diminished seventh chord ([1] 0:52) in the bass. This time the resolution comes in a minor chord ([1] 1:04). A different, more frantically insistent figure ([1] 1:09) is then heard in another rise and fall. Answering it ([1] 1:22) is a short cascade of notes followed by a marching rhythm, which are repeated, punctuated by a sudden virtuosic run up the keyboard, and repeated again. Two chords ([1] 1:41) seem to bring relief, but another virtuosic run puts an end to that with a plunge into another diminished seventh chord ([1] 1:49). A frenzy breaks out that eventually collects itself into a series of chords ([1] 2:06), but they founder on a fierce, descending echo of the opening and surrender to the darkness of a slowly resolving minor chord ([1] 2:23). After a pause, the fugue begins ([1] 2:32).

A fugue presents the counterpoint of different voices (or individual lines) that enter successively in imitation of the first voice, which presents the fugue's subject. The staggered layering of these voices in the introductory passage, or exposition, is what gives the fugue its complex but integrated sound. A fugue can take a number of shapes and forms. This fugue, which begins with a simple, undulating subject, grows in richness in its exposition until the voices include the organ's pedal ([1] 3:43). Bach develops the material in interesting ways, such as employing "echo" effects ([1] 4:06) that reflect the imitative nature of the fugue's exposition ([1] 5:20). After a vigorous workout, the fugue finally comes to rest on a surprising major chord ([1] 7:27). The concluding toccata section erupts ([1] 7:32), and eventually lands on yet another diminished seventh chord that unfolds and resolves itself in a major chord ([1] 8:05) in a highly ambiguous manner. Another brilliant, virtuoso outburst ([1] 8:09) reaches a higher plateau ([1] 8:21), but still aspires—almost panting—before the resolve fades into the dark resolution of a minor chord.

English Suite No. 1 in A, BWV 806. Along with the companion *French Suites,* the *English Suites* are among the most significant keyboard works Bach wrote. There are six of them, probably composed around the time Bach was serving as organist and chamber musician at the court of Duke Wilhelm Ernst of the German city-state of Weimar in 1715. They were published as early as 1726 in Leipzig, and then reissued in 1731, along with the *French Suites* and the six Partitas, in the *Clavier-Übung* volumes.

A musical form from the Baroque and Classical eras, suite describes a work in several movements, each of which is based on a dance. Its origin is French, as the movement titles indicate. Interestingly, Bach never applied the labels *French* and *English* to his two sets of keyboard suites. The term *French Suite* is redundant, while the *English Suites* are so named because one copy from Bach's time (there is no autograph manuscript) contains the words *"Fait pour les Anglois"* ("Made for the English"). In fact, there is nothing English about them. Each of the six *English Suites* begins with a substantial prélude*;* the second, third, fourth, and sixth movements are identical in style and called, respectively, an allemande, a courante, a sarabande, and a gigue; and the fifth movement is always a set of contrasted dances, either a bourrée, a gavotte, a minuet, or a passepied. The forms themselves are simple and do not require extensive commentary; it is Bach's dazzling imagination in full flight that makes them so magnificent.

From **Gigue**

A prélude is simply an introductory piece. This one (Band No. 2) begins with ripple of arpeggios that suddenly descends into the principal melody (2 0:05), a subject so rich and plangent that one can imagine it as being written for the organ. The left hand echoes the melody in the right as Bach elaborates on and develops its opening phrase of descending notes. The allemande (Band No. 3), probably a dance of German origin, is serious but not ponderous, and played at a moderate tempo. The courante (Band No. 4) is a French dance played at a moderate tempo; the Italians cast it in triple meter (in 3, like a waltz), the French in duple (in 2, like a polka). In this particular movement, Bach expands the presentation to a pair of courantes. Courante I is contrasted with Courante II (4 0:57), followed by two doubles that are variations, respectively, on the themes of each courante (4 2:05 and 4 3:12). The sarabande (Band No. 5) is a slow, dignified dance that perhaps was brought back to Spain from Mexico in the sixteenth century. The bourrée (Band No. 6) is a lively seventeenth-century French dance, probably from the Auvergne region, that the seventeenth-century French composer Jean-Baptiste Lully popularized in his ballets and operas. In this movement Bach uses two bourrées (the second beginning at 6 0:59), returning ultimately to the first (6 1:43). The gigue (Band No. 7), a Continental version of the high-spirited Irish or English jig, served as a standard finale in the typical suite of Bach's time. Typically, this gigue is exuberant and brief, a kind of musical exclamation point.

PARTITA NO. 5 IN G, BWV 629. Bach's most sophisticated use of the suite form is evident in the six Partitas for keyboard, written after his move to Leipzig in 1723. They were published together in 1731 in the first volume of the *Clavier-Übung*, which Bach indicated was "composed for Music-Lovers for the Refreshment of their Spirits."

The Italian word *partita* means "variation." The various movements of the musical suite of dances known as the partita are usually not variations on a theme, but, as in the case of Bach's G Major Partita, display a consistency of mood and temper that each movement reflects differently. The order and nature of the movements correspond to that of the *English Suites,* though there are seven movements instead of six. Here the Italian influence is more dominant than the French. (Note the use of Italian forms in some of the movement titles.) The sprightly Italian *corrente* seems to have won over Bach, who previously used its more sedate French form, the courante, as his model. The sparkling *Praembulum* (Band No. 8), with its neatly cascading lines splashing down delightfully, opens the partita in a jaunty, debonair manner that continues to the end of the movement. The allemande (Band No. 9) is richly expressive; the melody's gentle curves are beautifully displayed in this recording on a modern concert grand piano. A contrasting section follows (⑨2:24) the repeat (⑨1:10) of the principal melody, which eventually works its way back into the action before the movement comes to an end with a beguiling touch (⑨3:58) that serves as a tiny coda. The corrente (Band No. 10) has a delicately festive air that reflects the exuberance of the Italian music of the day that Bach so admired. The sarabande (Band No. 11) brings a brief, but unhurried period of introspection and poetic calm that does not disrupt the partita's overall genial mood. It is a perfect example of Bach's uncanny ability to clearly define the melody's rhythmic contours and keep them moving forward, while also achieving a sensuous, expressive line. The *tempo di minuetto* (Band No. 12) retains the courtly air of the minuet while pursuing a kind of quiet brilliance. The passepied (Band No. 13) is modeled after a vigorous French dance of the same name, originally from Brittany, that was popular in the court of King Louis XIV. After the restraint of the *tempo di minuetto,* it seems extroverted and physical. The gigue (Band No. 14) is the longest movement in this partita, dominated by its odd, comically abrupt opening figure. A second theme arrives (14 2:06), full of trills. The counterpoint suddenly becomes dizzyingly abuzz with these trills, all commented on by the ever-reiterated opening figure.

"LITTLE" FUGUE IN G MINOR, BWV 678. After the writhing fugue section in the middle of the Toccata and Fugue in D Minor, the brief Fugue in G Minor (which probably dates from the same period) charms with its clarity and compact ingenuity. This fugue is defined by a simple clockwork melody in three parts (beginning at 15 0:01, 0:08, and 0:14), after which subsidiary voices enter (at 15 0:17, 0:40, and 0:57). Proceeding like a well-oiled machine, the combination of voices rises to a sublime moment of gently rippling calm (15 3:11), which continues to climb with increasing power until the fugue's original subject emerges again clearly in the bass and marches the whole work home in the final embrace of a major chord.

A few words are in order about this performance, which contains wrong notes and an occasionally faltering tempo. Albert Schweitzer, the great humanitarian, made this recording in 1935 at All Hallows by the Tower in London, the first of a

Title page of the first volume of the Clavier-Übung, *published in 1731.*

series of recordings of Bach's organ music he made with EMI Records under the direction of Walter Legge. At that time Schweitzer relied on his virtuosity as an organist to raise money for his primary medical work in Africa. As a result, his playing is inconsistent, and its style is frequently at odds with modern scholarship about the performance of Bach on the organ. This recording and the others Schweitzer made in 1936–37 are profoundly moving, however, in that they speak of a devotion to Bach's music that—together with Schweitzer's landmark biography of the composer—led to a more sophisticated approach to Bach scholarship and performance.

ITALIAN CONCERTO IN F MINOR, BWV 971. Bach himself called this unique work *Concerto nach Italienischen Gusto (Concerto in the Italian Style* or *Italian Concerto)*. With *Overture in the French Style,* BWV 831, it constitutes the second volume of Bach's *Clavier-Übung (Keyboard Practice),* a collection of keyboard pieces published in 1735. Other *Clavier-Übung* volumes contain the six Partitas, the French and English suites, and the *Goldberg Variations.*

The *Italian Concerto* may seem curious because it is a concerto in which the single instrument is both soloist and accompanist; there is no orchestra. Like the Partitas and the Suites, this work—in its broad expressiveness—might be considered a prototypical solo sonata. (The solo sonata as we know it would come into its own only with Haydn and Mozart, decades after Bach's death in 1750.) He used the means at his disposal, playing with the Italian concerto style and format in this work for a solo keyboard instrument. The richness of the writing here suggests that he was beginning to push for a more expressive range from the instrument, and it calls for a harpsichord with two, rather than one, manual keyboards.

Despite the Germanic influences on his music, Bach admired the Italian masters, particularly Corelli and Vivaldi, and modeled his work after theirs. The *Italian Concerto* is in three compact movements in a typical fast-slow-fast configuration: an allegro, an andante, and a presto. The allegro (Band No. 16) begins with a vivid, forthright melody that behaves much like the accompanying ensemble (the *ripieno*) in an Italian *concerto grosso*. A contrasting passage (16 0:36) of a more delicate nature suggests the role of the soloists (the *concertante* or the *soli*) in the *concerto grosso*. The more forceful voice of the *ripieno* returns (16 1:03), developing the material heard in the first section. Bach's brilliant, muscular writing is built upon contrasting passages of music, differing in dynamics and texture, as the harpsichord, by its very nature, is incapable of varied tonal color or subtlety. The density of the writing lightens for a lengthy, virtuoso solo passage (16 2:03) before the block chords of the *ripieno* come crashing down again (16 3:14), leading to an almost orchestral conclusion. The beautiful andante (Band No. 17) begins with chords and a droning bass note that serve as a melancholy accompaniment for the principal theme (17 0:16), a long-flowing subject, improvisatory in nature, resembling an aria or the kind of melody Vivaldi or Corelli would assign the oboe. Its second strain (17 1:10)—warmer, slightly more fluent, and open—ends in an assured trill (17 2:32). The pensive mood of the opening statement returns in the melody (17 2:39), its intensity rising as it twists and turns. The song seems to exhaust itself with a trill (17 4:18), but continues until the final, wistful strain quietly fades away. The zesty presto (Band No. 18) opens with solid and joyous sounds like those of an orchestra, dancing with a sly, rhythmic swagger before the solo voice enters (18 0:24). It continues in the spirit of the opening, echoing the principal melody, before giving way to a disarming section in which the harpsichord's sound is dampened ([18] 1:14). Its native brilliance returns ([18] 1:28), continuing to develop and explore the melodic material with increasing intensity and contrast (such as the brief passage beginning at [18] 2:02). The forceful melody of the opening bars breaks through again ([18] 2:26), leading a headlong rush toward the finish, which it reaches with a contented sigh.

Albert Schweitzer, the great humanitarian, was also a pivotal force in Bach scholarship.

The Performers

Wanda Landowska (1879–1959) helped reintroduce the harpsichord into the performance of Classical music in the early decades of the twentieth century. Born in Poland and educated there as a pianist, Landowska began concertizing as a harpsichordist in 1903 and eventually settled in Paris. Her performance of Bach on original instruments was unusual at the time—his keyboard music, for instance, was then invariably performed on modern concert grand pianos, with a thick overlay of Romantic interpretation. Incarcerated by the Germans in Berlin during World War I, Landowska returned to France and established a school for the study of early music near Paris, at St.-Leu-la-Forêt, where she also built a concert hall and produced concerts of early music. (The recording of the *Italian Concerto* heard here was made at St.-Leu-la-Forêt in 1935–36.) World-renowned as a harpsichordist, Landowska also commissioned new works for the instrument from the celebrated composers Falla and Poulenc. When Germany invaded France, she was forced to flee, leaving behind her school, library, and fabulous collection of harpsichords. She arrived in New York in 1941, settling in Connecticut and teaching there for the rest of her life. Landowska is considered the mother of the original-instruments movement. Her performances are as noted for their interpretive flair as for their authenticity.

The Italian organist **Fernando Germani (b. 1906)** began his rise to prominence while a student at Rome's Accademia di Santa Cecilia, where he studied with Ottorino Respighi, among others. After a brief stint on the faculty of Philadelphia's Curtis Institute of Music, Germani returned to Italy. He served as organist at St. Peter's in Rome from 1947 until 1959 and toured internationally thereafter.

The Dutch-born **Gustav Leonhardt (b. 1928)** has found equal fame as an organist, harpsichordist, conductor, and teacher. Educated in Basel and Vienna, he made his debut in Vienna as a harpsichordist in 1950 and later served as a professor of harpsichord at that city's Academy of Music. In 1954 he moved his base of operations to the Amsterdam Conservatory. Leonhardt has toured and recorded extensively as a harpsichordist and as conductor of the Leonhardt Consort, an early-music group. He has also edited significant editions of the music of Baroque and early Classical composers, including a definitive edition of Bach's *Die Kunst der Fuge (The Art of the Fugue)*.

Maria Tipo (b. 1931)

Maria Tipo (b. 1931) is an Italian pianist and teacher who has shaped her career according to the repertoire she liked, not according to the expectations of the musical world. As a young woman she won a number of international prizes and concertized widely in the 1950s, though the narrow focus of her repertoire limited her exposure. Not widely known until the 1980s, when her recordings garnered an enthusiastic international audience, she has always been a connoisseur's favorite, especially in the performance of Bach and the early Italian keyboard masters Scarlatti and Clementi. Her insistence on using a piano (instead of a historically correct harpsichord, clavichord, or fortepiano) makes her performance of Bach somewhat of an anomaly today, though her cultivated manner and subtle command of his challenging repertoire are virtually without equal.

Albert Schweitzer (1875–1965) was an Alsatian-born man for all seasons— theologian, philosopher, medical missionary, organist, and musical scholar. The son of a Lutheran pastor, Schweitzer decided early on to devote the first part of his life to philosophy and art, the second to action. He studied organ and music theory in Strasbourg, while also studying for the ministry. When he began his medical studies in Strasbourg, he was organ soloist with the city's Bach Concerts series and later took the same position with the Bach Society in Paris. In 1913 Schweitzer went to Africa to establish the hospital that became the focus of his life. He made many trips back to Europe to play Bach concerts, primarily to raise money for his hospital. One of the twentieth century's most admired humanitarians, he was awarded the Nobel Peace Prize in 1952. He remains the only professional musician to be so honored. His biography of Bach, first published in 1905, was a major event in Bach scholarship, and his ideas about Bach's life and music had a profound effect on the rebirth of interest in both during the twentieth century.

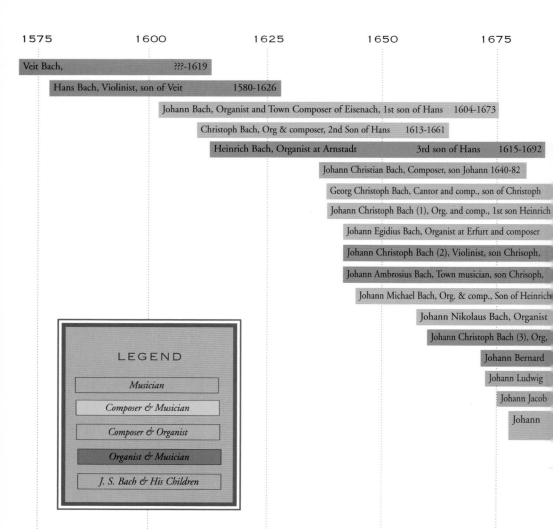

1575	1600	1625	1650	1675

Veit Bach, ???-1619

Hans Bach, Violinist, son of Veit   1580-1626

Johann Bach, Organist and Town Composer of Eisenach, 1st son of Hans   1604-1673

Christoph Bach, Org & composer, 2nd Son of Hans   1613-1661

Heinrich Bach, Organist at Arnstadt   3rd son of Hans   1615-1692

Johann Christian Bach, Composer, son Johann 1640-82

Georg Christoph Bach, Cantor and comp., son of Christoph

Johann Christoph Bach (1), Org. and comp., 1st son Heinrich

Johann Egidius Bach, Organist at Erfurt and composer

Johann Christoph Bach (2), Violinist, son Chrisoph,

Johann Ambrosius Bach, Town musician, son Chrisoph,

Johann Michael Bach, Org. & comp., Son of Heinrich

Johann Nikolaus Bach, Organist

Johann Christoph Bach (3), Org,

Johann Bernard

Johann Ludwig

Johann Jacob

Johann

LEGEND

Musician

Composer & Musician

Composer & Organist

Organist & Musician

J. S. Bach & His Children

| 1700 | 1725 | 1750 | 1775 | 1800 |

The Bach Family Timeline

There were at least fifty-three members of the Bach family who were musicians and/or composers over seven generations and three hundred years. Here are some of them.

1642-1697

1642-1703

2nd son of Johann 1645-1717

1645-1694

1645-1695

1648-1694

at Jena & composer, eldest son of Johann Christoph (1)   1669-1753

teacher J. S. Bach, son of J. A. 1671-1721

Bach, Organist & court musician, son Johann Egidius 1676-1749

Bach, comp. & musician, son of J.Michael 1677-1730

Bach, comp. & musician, son of J. A.   1682-1730

Sebastian Bach, org. and comp., 8th son of Johann Ambrosius Bach
1685-1750

Wilhelm Friedman Bach, "Halle Bach," organist & composer, Eldest son of J. S. Bach
1710- 1784

Carl Philip Emanuel Bach, composer, Court harpsichordist to Frederick the Great,
5th child, 2nd son of J. S. Bach   1714-1788

Johann Christoph Friedrich Bach, "Bückeberg Bach," comp. & musical
director, 9th son of J. S. Bach   1732-1795

Johann Christian Bach, "English Bach," Master of Music to
King George III, 18th child, 11th son of J. S. Bach 1735-1782